Sandy Jeffs is the author and co-author of two prize-winning books of poetry. Her writing has been concerned with a range of subjects, including madness, domestic violence and midweek tennis. She divides her time between writing poetry, playing midweek tennis and speaking to community groups about mental illness. Sandy lives with her friends and animals on a property just out of Melbourne.

Also By Sandy Jeffs

Poems from the Madhouse

Loose Kangaroos (co-author)

Confessions of a Midweek Lady (forthcoming)

Blood Relations

Sandy Jeffs

Spinifex Press Pty Ltd
504 Queensberry Street
North Melbourne, Vic. 3051
Australia
women@spinifexpress.com.au
http://www.spinifexpress.com.au

First published by Spinifex Press, 2000
Copyright © Sandy Jeffs, 2000
Copyright © on page layout and design: Spinifex Press, 2000

Cover design by Deb Snibson, Modern Art Production Group
Edited by Patricia Sykes
Typeset in Souvenir by Palmer Higgs
Made and printed in Australia by Australian Print Group

This project has been assisted by the
Commonwealth Government through the
Australia Council, its arts funding and advisory
body.

National Library of Australia
Cataloguing-in-Publication data:
Jeffs, Sandy, 1953– .
    Blood relations.
    ISBN 1 875559 98 1.
    I. Title.

A821.4

For my
brother and sister

Acknowledgements

These poems had their origins in a family history of
domestic violence and alcoholism. I was able to explore
the emotions behind these poems because I was
privileged to be surrounded by loving friends who lived
through these poems with me. I thank Robbie and Dido
for the love, the space, and the home they gave me,
without which these poems would never have seen the
light of day. To Lynne and Felicity, who saw many of
these poems in their various incarnations and offered lots
of helpful comments, I thank you for the support and
enduring friendship. To the many others who have
helped me along the way, thank you. Patricia Sykes was
the editor from heaven. Her incisive and detailed reading
of the poems helped me distance myself from my
emotional involvement in the subject and allowed the
poet to speak. I would like to thank Susan Hawthorne
and Renate Klein at Spinifex Press for giving these
poems the chance to reach a wider audience.

The author thanks the following copyright holders for
permission to quote from the works cited:
Anna Akhmatova, lines from 'Requiem' in *Twentieth
Century Russian Poetry* introduced by Yevgeny
Yevtushenko and edited by Albert Todd and Max
Hayward, Fourth Estate, London, 1994.
Sherryl Clarke, lines from 'Driving Down Gravel Pit
Road', and 'An Archeology of Self' from *Thicker Than
Water*, Pariah Press, Melbourne, 1999.

Contents

Immaculate Deception

Crazy Woman Survivor

Since then, at an uncertain hour,
That agony returns:
And till my ghastly tale is told,
This heart within me burns.

Samuel Taylor Coleridge

From the Cradle

Holding back
from the hurts of childhood
doesn't let you travel more freely...

Sherryl Clark

JEFFS (nee Bryant)—on
July 15. at Intermediate,
to Mavis and Max—a
daughter, (Sandra).

Obsession

You weigh heavily on my mind
poems ooze out of me about you
it's an obsession
I want the world to know
how awful it was
I want to exorcise my bitterness
I want to tell the children I never had
not to do what you did
not to feel as I feel now
not to let anger steel their hearts
you weigh heavily on my mind
and I don't know what to do
except write poems of love and hate.

Recollections in Melancholy

These cloying moments,
of the inward journey backwards, cling—
the ghoulish details
the unsummoned visitations
the unquiet feelings
the churning guts
the breathless cries
the fun times subsumed
by thoughts that are not forgotten
in the mire of melancholy.

Thoughts drive my pen
these unyielding memories
of a family in despair—
my memory frenetic with
what I do not want to remember
reminiscing in an eternal now
seeing the power of his hand
and the glint in his eye
smelling the waft of her beery breath
and all the sadness welling
sobbing into my pillow
the world turned upside down—
a child's emotion
recollected in melancholy.

Centre Stage

You ask me to state
exactly
what I remember
like some attendant
in theatre
relating incisions

Tracy Ryan

Sometimes memory warps
cobbling together a host of images
leaving the self
embellished by the past.

In this memory you are centre stage
in an Edward Albee play
his Martha and George tearing each other apart
victim and perpetrator of an Inquisition.

I remember too much
a warp that sustains me.
I incise too deeply
seeing more than I should;
you lie on the table
bleeding my memories.

Australian Dream

Someone told me I chose my parents.
I wouldn't have chosen so badly
chosen such misery if I had known.
I must have done bad things
in a previous life
unspeakable, unforgivable
to have created so much bad Karma.

Like all postwar families
we clung to an ideal
that never was
the ideal *we* tried to be part of
the Australian Dream
in a provincial city
in our brick house
doing family things
like going to the golf club or the pub
sitting in the two-tone green FJ
while Dad brought out sarsaparillas saying:
we won't be long
while time dragged on and on
and the sleazy man walking past saying:
close your legs luv
I'll get back to you when you're older
and me blushing with shame;
years later riding like royalty
in the new two-tone brown EH
that ferried me to my sports
where Mum and Dad barracked enthusiastically
proud of my achievements
sport a passion that saved my life.

That was how it was then
in a provincial city
with nothing to do
making our own fun
never talking about
politics, sex or religion;
going to Sunday School
to learn about the all-loving Father
Heaven and Hell and Holy Ghosts
secretly wondering whether we weren't
already living in Hell;
never conversing with the *New Australians*
except when we bought fish and chips
from the Greeks at the corner shop
wondering about the fate
of the children of mixed marriages because
you couldn't mix blood or blend religions
and anyway the *Micks* had guns
in the crypts of their churches
the *Commies* were gonna get us
and *Pig Iron Bob* was God
so Dad said.

In our provincial city
we were self-destructing before
the gaze of the whole town
where gossip was rife
and everything was reported in the local rag
even Mum's drunken driving
and she the first woman charged
and me trying to act as though
nothing had happened.

We imploded in our own home
went into a nosedive
behind the walls of the bunker.
I'm sure the neighbours
could hear the screams
and Dad's unrelenting anger
bashing Mum:
where have you been!?
Him cycling around the lake
to catch her with other men
even though I saw him kissing
another woman in the backyard;
Mum drinking herself into oblivion
saying back at him: *I've been out!*
never saying where she'd been
me never understanding her secrecy
but remembering my disappointment
when I saw her kissing
a strange man in a car park:
don't tell Daddy, these things happen
and every weekend ramming the gates
drunk at the wheel of the EH
which we called The Concertina
because it had had so many bingles.

I wrestled the agony
and stifled my fears
while dreaming of another life
one that I would have chosen
like living with Miss Vines
my favourite teacher
or just to be somewhere else
where I could be happy

as I sat on the tram
in that cold provincial city
on the way to school
wondering about the madness
in which I lived
the madness I didn't choose.

I couldn't have foreseen
what Mum and Dad would leave in their wake
like my sister trying to create
the family she never had
my brother fearing himself to distraction
both still living in that provincial city
which I had to flee to tame the ghouls.
I couldn't have foreseen
how a briar would entwine itself around my heart
nor could I have foreseen
how I would plunge into a different madness
which I didn't choose either
where my mind vanishes into a vortex.

No one could have foreseen
how we would bare the scars
in hushed tones and strangled words
how darkly we would view the world
how our lives would ebb and never flow
how we would welcome the reaping
of their turbulent lives
and begin the long walk back.

Happy Family

In this house I am home again
inside the familiar contradiction...

Sherryl Clark

Wedding Day Smiles

Dad always said
the hardest part of his wedding
though he didn't mind
was all the smiling he had to do for the cameras—
official photographers organising the wedding party
friends and rellies clicking away
to record the special moments like
the arrival, the confetti, the tears,
the exchange of vows, the smiles.

Then there were the milling many
who turned up just to see the bride
emerge radiant from the church smiling
as joyous bells peeled for the joyous occasion.
It was a happy day.

O the celebrations were wildly happy.
Partying on well into the night after the reception
they all went back to the family home.
Mum's brothers had stashed a keg in the washhouse
and gallons of champagne in the troughs
even though Mum's fierce mother Kate
a teetotaller had forbidden it.
The grog flowed like untapped waters:
it was a ripsnorter of a turn
everyone getting sloshed except Kate.
Mum and Dad wiped-out by night's end
finally collapsing into a mourning coach
(borrowed from Uncle Ted
who worked for an undertaker)
which took them to Melbourne

for the beginning of their honeymoon—
Mum in her merriment forgetting her honeymoon bags
Uncle Wal making a mercy dash
next morning in the vegetable truck.

It must have been outrageously delicious
to see everyone with smiles on their faces
as broad as the Sydney Harbour Bridge.
It was a wedding to be remembered.

On Looking at a Wedding Photo
of Max and Mavis

Mother:
Did he court you with flowers and chocolates?
Did he whisper sweet nothings in your ear?
Did he woo you with passion?
Did he promise to be there in sickness and in health?
Did he promise never to anger and rage?
Did he promise never to beat you?
Did he promise never to humiliate you?
Did he promise never to seek anyone else?
Did he promise anything?
                    Were all his promises lies?

Father:
Did she court you with flowers and chocolates?
Did she whisper sweet nothings in your ear?
Did she woo you with passion?
Did she promise to be there in sickness and in health?
Did she promise to accept your anger and rage?
Did she promise to accept your beatings?
Did she promise never to humiliate you?
Did she promise never to seek anyone else?
Did she promise anything?
                    Were all her promises lies?

Are you both still raging and fighting
in your death-house of broken promises?

To the happy couple...hooray.

Façade

We played happy family
presented ourselves as *normal*
sanitised our image
deluded ourselves with lies.
Something was rotting in our family.

Playing happy family
was a full time job.
Going to school
with the screams and punches
playing themselves over in my mind
while pretending to be happy
was a killer.
Something was rotting in our family.

Mum stayed indoors for days
powdered her bruised face
nursed her battered body
sent me on messages
made up excuses.
He brought her cups of coffee
pretended nothing had happened.
Something was rotting in our family.

Yet still I pretended to be happy.
In the end my heart watched
in dazed disbelief
while my family rotted
knowing no one could smell the stench.

Vespers

Now I lay me down to sleep.
Sleep was broken
by the noises that
came from their room.
Something was going to happen.
Indeed, sleep did not come
with the tension in the air
the hate, the bitterness
the night about to explode
with the warring factions
hounding each other with slurs.
The fearful child whispered:
I pray the Lord my soul to keep.

Gentle Jesus meek and mild.
Then the night howled
with the screams of anger
and the darkness was punctuated
by the outbursts of violence.
There, amidst the smashed crockery
the telephone wrenched from the wall
the splashes of blood on the cupboards
in the deathly quiet of the aftermath
the child prayed:
Look upon this little child.

If I should die before I wake.
The morning after was plagued
by unanswered questions
the unspoken words between them
that let the events of the night

seep into a sinister silence.
Nothing had happened
it was all in her imagination
the invention of a wilful child.
Her mother's bruises were not real.
She had not heard their
abusive, accusatory words
or witnessed the body blows
or felt the earth shatter
into piercing shards of hatred.
The nightmare was uglier than Hell
and it rankled her soul
until she wailed:
I pray the Lord my soul to take.

You Lived Life to Death

You both lived life to death
in a way only you could
taking the world with you
taking hostages like deranged
terrorists intent on a death-fix.

Outrageous as always—
the booze, the violence, the life-style
the dead-end, disgusting relationship—
you had it all
it was bad and it was ugly.

I cannot think of anything good
about your collective wills—
death was the toy
with which you played.
In the end, you snared it
like a myxo rabbit
dying before your respective times.

I wonder about bitterness.
I wonder more about bitter pills—
the taste is not so sweet.
Memory is locked
like a stylus stuck in
the groove of a scratched record
repeating flashbacks
unbearable reminders
of your hateful conflicts.

Together you were monsters
on a self-destructive path
trapping me in a prison
of self-doubt
unable to fend off life.

O yes, you lived life to death
but left me to live a deathly life.

Lament

I spent my childhood years
cowering in the corner while you fought.

I spent my teenage years
looking for someone to replace you.

I spent my adult years
avoiding you.

I spend your post-death years
trying to understand your absence
and the love we did not have.

We were always strangers
even at my conception.
The fruit of your union
became the estranged child
and anguished adult
who despairs at the hollowness
of our hapless lives.
I never did know you
yet I wanted to know you so badly
that the ache of my heart
cuts a savage swathe.

If your ashes could speak
dare I ask the question?
If you stood before me as
the man and woman you once were
could you tell me who you are?
I ask too much.

My regret should not disturb your slumber
even if it keeps me from mine.
Indeed, I spend your post-death years
awash with flighty feelings
I can barely contain
and lament what we did not share.

The Mourning After

The morning's calm suddenly howled
with the crashing sounds of the
pots being thrown about the cupboards—
he was up.
There was no mistaking
his temper tirade
as he made it known he
was preparing his breakfast.
World War III entered and left
the kitchen every morning
with the dead left to rot
on the sink in the baking sun
after he had sated himself
on his fat-oozing bacon and eggs
that mingled with the juices
of stale beer and cigarettes
in his filthy mouth.

Their room reeked of it.

Later in the morning
in the fraught quiet
after he had gone
she would pull herself from the bed
slip on her dressing-gown
and make her way down the slender passage
showing no visible signs
of the drunkenness of the night before.

Taking a glass of water
she would throw down a *Bex* powder
and survey the battle ground—
she was up.
There was no mistaking
her bruises and battered face
or trembling hands
that held the weak, black coffee.
She never said a word.
She didn't have to
it was the mourning after.

Bringing in the Washing

Sitting in the lounge room playing *Family*
the pretence was gruelling.
Mum and Dad
in front of the cosy fire
he reading the *Reader's Digest*
she knitting.
We smiled wanly
talked cautiously
immersed ourselves in our
secret thoughts of escaping
while watching *The Nelsons* on TV.
We were an archipelago of misery
cyclone-battered islands
without jetties or lagoons
for boats to shelter from storms.

Sitting in the lounge room playing *Family*
it was a simple thing that
made the hatred disappear
and galvanised us for a moment.
When the light rain touched the roof
we, all of us, rushed outside.
We, together, picked the
clothes-clad *Hills Hoist* naked.
We, united, carried in the bundles.
We, consolidated by a purpose,
were no longer pretending.
I looked adoringly at Ossie and Harriet
engaged in their task,

the rain having washed
away their sneering hostility.
I spied my siblings' faces
showing a hint of relief.
The misery seemed far away
and all this through a simple thing
the thing to which
I always looked forward:
the days when the Nelsons
would bring in the washing.

Christmas Eve

As I lay on the couch
letting loose my imaginings
I saw others bursting with joy
eager for the morning's
unwrapping and fun.

As I lay on the couch
the stain of foreboding
crept over me.

Fear that she wasn't home yet.
Fear that he was waiting for her.
Fear that she would be drunk.
Fear that he would bash her.
Fear of the unknown.
Fear of the inevitable.
Fear of the fear.

The car hitting the gate
stirred him from the chair.
Like a bull beginning
to anger at the red cape
he stiffened his red face
and narrowed his eyes.

She staggered in.

He pounced.
She reeled.
He interrogated.
She screamed.
He bashed.
She fell.
He bashed.
She fell.
Time passed

Staggering through the house
throwing cellophane parcels
she cried out through tears:
I'm going to the lake!
He abused and ranted.
She left.
We wept.

The Silent Scream

After I had left
you in your silence
I was visited by a child
who had lain dormant.
She came to me in the
starkness of the day
and told me of a misery
that had eaten her soul
and rotted her life-force.
She retched and wailed
in my arms and I caressed
her convulsing torso
until a calm descended.
She told me of her memories
about a time when the world
was a fretful place
how she would pray for love
to embrace her cold heart.
She told me of her abandonment
and her withdrawal into herself.
She told me of her scream that
was never heard by them
over their cacophony of horror.

The scream continues today.
It is silent and inward now
tearing to shreds the inner world
that makes meaning out of the myriad
events that touch one along the way.

When I left you in your silence
the silent scream of a child filled
my ears and reminded me of a past
to which I am fettered forever.

The Silence of the Lambs

Shorn of our wool
laid bare for the vultures' talons
not even the tar on our wounds
could stem the flow
and we bled and bled
in silence.

Silence is golden

In loyalty we uttered nothing
choked on what we witnessed
children struck dumb
unable to tell the terror
and we bled and bled
in silence.

Silence is golden

We cursed the house of horrors
we lived in endless fear
our lives were shackled
to a nightmare we dare not name
and we bled and bled
in silence.

Silence is golden

Lambs waiting for the slaughter
we bled and bled
in silence.

Silence is golden

Silence is

Silence

In Sullied Silence We Drowned

In sullied silence we drowned
Our fractured lives betrayed
Trying to utter a sound
We lived our lives afraid.

Our fractured lives betrayed
We endured unbearable pain
We lived our lives afraid
Our hope for love was slain.

We endured unbearable pain
We whispered wordless prayers
Our hope for love was slain
We sang our mournful airs.

We whispered wordless prayers
We harboured hopes to flee
We sang our mournful airs
Like children lost at sea.

We harboured hopes to flee
Trying to utter a sound
Like children lost at sea
In sullied silence we drowned.

Crimson Memories

Fragments of an interlude—

memories thrust themselves
like skivers
goring the ventricles of my heart

my life haemorrhages because
blood is thicker than water

family blood gushed gallons
the sluicegates could not hold
the blood so thin
guttered down the gully trap

floods of innocence washed away
in a crimson cascade

collected memories are stained with blood

Fragments of an interlude—

memories remind me
of my haemophilic family
which bled to death.

Fork in the Road

When did we take
the fork in the road
that led us to the
house of menace?

When did we descend
into the dark room
where we became strangers
lost in each other's darkness?

Privately Cremated

he wouldn't let me sleep/ he
wouldn't leave me alone to dream/ a child's
dreams

Coral Hull

Mein Führer

The Night of Long Knives: September 1971

Mein Führer,
when I stumbled into the
pregnant quiet of the
remains of your ambush,
the walls and cupboards
splattered red
furniture overturned
shards of crockery everywhere,
I quaked with fright
reeled in terror
thought you'd killed her
didn't want to know anything
went into a daze
just had to leave.
Numbed to my bones
yet my heart pounding
I ran into the street
needed to talk to someone.
Frantic, I found a telephone
and rang Directory Assistance:
sorry, Lifeline won't be
connected until next month.
Sat in the gutter and wailed
too scared to go back.
Hid like a Jew in the Fatherland
wandered the cold streets
an orphan of the Reich.

On My Return

Mein Führer,
for a week of a thousand nights
you huddled over a piddling fire
that warmed your rage
while you kept her in the
coldest corner of the room—
as cold as the iceberg
that pumped hatred through
your bloodless veins.
You ripped the telephone
out of the wall
trashed the kitchen
locked the doors
beat her senseless
tortured her like a spy
in the hands of
your Gestapo cronies
picked over her carcass
like your SS henchmen
looking for gold fillings.

Liberation

Mein Führer,
she left you
stealing away one night
when you dropped your guard
taking her bruises and welts
her black eyes and
trembling body with her.
She stole into the night
cutting the wire

pacifying your curs
dodging the lights
and fled your prison.

Mein Kampf

One day I will
relinquish the memories
forget the violence
obliterate the angry words
block out the flashbacks
kill the sadness that lingers
cut out the tumour
erase what I witnessed.
One day I will
bury the coffin containing
the remains of this time.
One day I will
bury you forever
Mein Führer, forever.

The S.A. (*Sturmabteilung*, storm troopers), known as the Brownshirts,
was a private army led by Earnst Roehm which helped Hitler to power
in 1933. It was soon seen as a threat by Hitler, so he prepared a trap
which would ultimately destroy them. Whilst meeting at Bad Wiessee, a
summer resort, Roehm and his leaders were murdered in their sleep by
the S.S.(*Schutzstaffel*) the Blackshirts, another private army, involved
in a power struggle with the S.A. This purge removed the S.A. from the
political scene. It became known as *The Night of Long Knives*, June
29 to July 2 1934.

She Came Back

Bye, baby bunting,
Daddy's gone a-hunting...

With your hell-hole empty
you set out to get Mum back.
Phone calls to my sister
interrogating viciously:
where's that bitch?
She told and soon you were
making journeys eastward
to the big smoke
taking Mum flowers
chocolates, presents
an even temper
and gentle hands.
You carried her off to love-nests
where you lusted and appeased.

I don't know why
she came back.
On her first night home
you bashed her again.

And he'll beat you, beat you, beat you,
And he'll beat you all to pap...

You Took Her

You took her
crushing her paper wings.

You took her
smothering her sobs.

You took her
after beating her.

You took her
after abusing her.

You took her
in twisted lust.

You took her
in blind rage.

You took her
without consent.

You took her!
You took her!

Daddy, when you took Mummy
you took me.

Every Friday Night

Every Friday night
you lie in wait
eyeing your prey
craving a carcass.

Every Friday night
we await the mauling
praying for intercession
that never comes.

Every Friday night
your savage moods
shroud us in dread
steal us of joy.

Every Friday night
in she walks
senses numbed
to endure your devouring of flesh.

Every Friday night
we visit the shades below
as you cut our hearts into pieces
tossing the bleeding bits to your cur
that guards the gate—
every inexorable Friday night.

Loony Bin

Mad Scene

Come and see them you said
come and see the loonies in the loony bin
where you blow your sax
and make sweet music
amidst this Hogarthian gathering
of misfits and freaks.
Your lips curled with a
cruel mirth as you spoke
and I was eager to see the show
to indulge my voyeuristic impulses
and see the loonies perform their antics
and talk their crazy talk.
Come and see them you said
and I did.

I stood on stage and looked down
you blew your sax
the music melted into the
dingy hall's fading walls
and the loonies danced
to their off-beat drums
and sang their off-key songs.
I laughed with gusto at the show
full of wonderful characters—
like the woman dressed as a frog
who waved to me all night;
the man who recited Shakespeare
and the loony who blew your sax
like an old trooper.

God, how I roared with laughter at the
mumbling, bumbling, drug-muddled mob
shuffling its lethargic waltz
slouching like anaesthetised snails.

But there were stories to be told
that added a mystique.
That man was a genius
before the chainsaw slashed his skull;
she sang in opera
before her nerves went;
he was a headmaster
before the car accident;
she painted like Da Vinci
before her mind shattered;
genius and madness are related you know,
so you said,
with awe in your voice.

It still didn't stop our laughter
as we dismissed their humanity
and betrayed our own.

Mad Irony

The wing of madness
casts a broad shadow.
It asks no favours
gives no warning
takes no hostages.
I became its prey
its spectre ambushing me
at one score and three.

I joined the mad chorus
sang mad songs
talked crazy talk
became a freak
shuffled a drug-wearied waltz
and my laughter ceased.

You came to see me once.
Your music had already soured
and now your laughter turned to denial:
ya don't believe what them
psychiatrists say, do ya?

In my loony bin wanderings
the faces I saw
were the same faces
I had laughed at with you.
Come and see them you said.
I did, and saw myself.
Who did you see, Dad?

I Have to Cleanse Myself of You

I have to cleanse myself of you
and your freakish ways
of your violent temper
and your black-hearted manner.

You belt her black and blue
and kick her to the ground.
Blind with rage you lash out
and torment with lust.
You disgust me beyond remorse.

Many are the times we drag you
away from her throat
and cry out: *please don't kill her!*
But all you hear is the crazed voice
in your black, crazed mind.

Every vitriolic word, every punch
leeches me of love's company.
I am ensnared in your savage world
a child caught in the Holocaust
your jackboots trampling me.

Shadowed by your demons
that pursue me to every hideaway I seek
I have to cleanse myself of you
or my soul will slowly starve
a withering vine never to bear fruit.

Deathbed Scene Remembrance

I came to your deathbed troubled
my heart cauterised to stop
the bleeding of the years
and saw you lying limp and languid
your heart barely beating
your life draining away.

I summoned from my depths
a feeble compassion
but as I looked on I only remembered
how your vexatious heart
pounded with cyclonic rage
battering us with its fury.
How could this be possible
as you lie child-like on the pillowed bed?

They tell me you are dying.
You lie there entwined
in the bedclothes and wires
clinging to life like a premature baby.
I cannot bring myself to touch you.
I stand back with the past engulfing me
awash with your demonic anger
the loveless life we endured
the distance I kept between us
that was never enough.

I thrash about in my
gossamer-shrouded shell
trying to untangle
this dreadful confusion.
Is this swaying of feelings
what death is about?
Do your dying then
and I shall contend with it!
But how lonely it is
how lonely the watching.

I left your deathbed
unable to gather you in my arms
unable to warm your chill in my heart.

The Pieta

You were lying in a vulnerable posture
oblivious, seemingly alone and fragile
your arms out to the side of your body
dangling over the barriers of the bed.
The body so slumped, so limp
so helpless
so near death.

But something transformed.
You were not alone
but held dearly by the Madonna
who caressed your racked, blue body
as though you were the Jesus of the Cross.
As ravaged in death's arms as you were
I could see you as an embodiment
of Michelangelo's *Pieta*.

I do not say this flippantly
but perhaps I am comforting myself with
an image of great art to assuage
my tumbling emotions which are grappling
with the dying and death of my part creator.

Yet I know what I saw and I ask:
did she caress you gently
wipe your brow and talk with you
through your morphine induced haze?
Did she tell you about Jesus' pain and death?
Does she caress everyone in their dying time?
Did she weep for you?

When I could not be with you to the last
I was happy to leave you
in the arms of the Madonna.

JEFFS, Keith Maxwell (Max)—Peacefully passed away, February 19, 1990. Loved husband of Mavis; loved father of Marilyn, Keith and Sandra; adored Grandpa of Brett, Jason and Fiona. Privately cremated on February 21.

Farewell to an Old Bastard

Keith Maxwell Jeffs
19/9/1920—19/2/1990

It's all over Dad,
and I am alone wondering
about this thing called grief.
The dying is done
and it wasn't an easy death
with you struggling,
keeping that jelly-thing-of-a-heart beating
just enough to grasp onto life at its end.
I did not want to deny you
your last struggle—
who could? who would?
It was hell watching and waiting.
Why didn't you let go sooner?

Numbed by imperious death's imminence,
I said a puzzled goodbye—
all I could muster was a faint: *see you*.
I fled your deathbed
not for the pain of watching
a loved one die
it was dealing with the unrelenting guilt
of enjoying your death that drove me away;
the relief of knowing you would
no longer be here to inflict your rages.
How I hankered to make a treaty
and dowse the fires of resentment.
(Secretly, though, I entertain the thought

that death is too good for you.)

But death, your slow, solitary dying
has not changed the essentials
and the piercing pain left
after years of your blistering anger
has severed my senses from life's delights.
In my confusion I think of your death
as a gift of sweet nectar.

Ashes to Ashes

And I see we are in
a dead people's place
where piles of ashes
rest in walls behind plaques
or are buried in garden-beds
that nurture rosebushes
which have prickles
to protect the blooming flowers.

Personally,
I would prefer a native to nestle
its searching roots
around your cold ashes
but I am a modern woman.

I do not think I like
your final resting place
nor even the idea that
you are a pile of ashes
which can be blown
away by a gentle breeze.
I am not even sure
I would want you to rot
in a grave and be
penetrated by worms.

Death is a problem for
those left behind;
the grieving is for us

who watch the dying
and are made mindful
of our own mortality.

Father, I would like to
think your ashes had senses
and you could receive our callings;
but death is death
matter to ashes
and we contemplate
with disbelief
your void.

Chalk Circle

The dead call from
the grave they say
a lilting song of beckoning.

Catherine roamed the moors
singing Heathcliff's name
until they dwelt together
beneath the earth
their *unquiet slumbers*
carried on the breath of the winds.

There is no meeting
on the moors for us
no wild souls seeking
each other's brooding love.
I leave you where you are
dead, a pile of ashes
your song lost to the flames;
a pile of ashes removed
from the casualties you left
strewn all around.

Stay away from my chalk circle!
My fortress of solitude.
You are removed
further from my senses
than even you could imagine.

I Will Not Burn With You

It was your death that
sent me into despair.
It is the waiting for mine
that unites us as desperate souls.

You call and call to me.
I teeter on the edge of your furnace.
Come! Come! you cry.
Come into the flames with your father.

Over and over you play the devil's trill
and I relent.
We are carried into the inferno
in our flower-crowned coffin
singing a dirge that fans the flames
which surge to lick our bodies—
I find myself entwined in your
swollen blue arms as you caress me.

In death you are unearthly
you beckon me like a beggar
but I will not go with you!
I will break away
from your inveigling fingers.
I will let you burn without me
and watch your flaccid heart melt.

Standing Stone

I stand before your coffin
stony and cold
while the mingling few
mourn your moment.

Absent from this place of mourning
I weather your death
like tall stones in the mist
refuse to crumble.

Standing stones do not weep
even though they carry great burdens.
I will stand a thousand years and more
and still be unmoved
standing solitary and tall in my strength.

One Year Later

i could hear my father's
voice invading my dreams/ i could almost
smell the poison that he placed inside/
me...

Coral Hull

All that stern year
the year after your death
your spectre haunted me.
Like a tigress protecting her young
I recoiled to protect myself
erecting barriers as high as heaven.
I did not know how to grieve
for your death which I had longed for.
It was a perverse joy that shadowed me.

Then the descent into hell
into the maelstrom of madness I fell
with *your* voice whispering in my ears
muddling my mind.

For weeks my mind screamed and squalled.
You hung over me like a rancid carcass
smothering me in your decay.
Shackled with your weights and chains
I longed for a calm night and long sleep
to cast you off to the sea's deep floor.

As the time neared I steadied.
Slumped in the day-room chair
I counted as the minutes
marched towards the moment.
On the stroke of your death
I felt something well in me.
I whispered to the nurse:
he's gone.
And I wept for the first time
even though the serpent of madness
was coiled around me in a deathly embrace.

Eulogy

I cannot laud your life
or utter a praiseworthy word
my throat is scoured
from an eternity of howling.
Yet, in your seething wake
the improbable prevails
and a little jewel pricks.
Your love of music shone bright
and as you wept unashamedly
in its resonant midst, it soothed you—
the monster was tamed.
I never understood this mystery
but I grasp it with all my senses.
Wherever you are
I hope the music is
singing to your soul—
this is all I have to hold of you.

Immaculate Deception

It is the incomplete,
The unfulfilled, the torn
That haunts our nights and days
And keeps us hunger-born.

May Sarton

Death in the Family

Uncle Ab's dead.
Uncle Charlie's dead.
Uncle Ec's dead
and Uncle Wal's in hospital with a growth.
Mother, your family is dying
and I wonder whether you'll be next.
I think about you
on your alcoholic tightrope
and your death defying act.

Uncle Wal is Dead

Uncle Wal is dead
and we are at the crematorium
watching his coffin disappear into the inferno.
Mother, your body quivers in its funeral rags
your gnarled hands tremble uncontrollably.
You too have given up life in your own way.

Father is next to you
and for a moment
all those years of your drunkenness
and his bashings, vanish
as he comforts you in his clumsy way.
But I stand alone
unable to summon pity and emotion
or lend my hand as solace.

You lose another brother
and I cannot bring myself
to lead you away from the
sorrow of death's calling.
Things might have been different
in another time and place.
Sometimes tragedy brings
families closer together
but our whole life was one tragedy
and my energy to love
was sucked dry years ago.

You Always Were Hard to Fathom

You always were hard to fathom—
made up of mixed spices
a complex equation
as elusive as the Pimpernel
but real beyond reality.

So much has been left unsaid
as though nothing ever happened
but it did, it did.
There were so many times when
the despair made me scream within.

The fights with him were too much to endure
your drunken behaviour too embarrassing
for the child who watched with sad eyes.
I loathe those times with a passion
and am glad to be away.

Yet there is no freedom for my soul
because all that went before lingers on
and I see you staggering through the years
unknowing of the shackles around my neck
and my silent prayers for your death.

You were blind to my waning love
given to substitutes who filled the gap
and my wounds wept out aloud
whilst many anguished cries
fell upon ears made deaf by drink.

Sometimes I feel for you though
for often a jewel shone through.
Honest and kind-hearted, they said.
And you always made a home for the
countless bedraggled strays I rescued.

But it was I who strayed away in the end
who ran from you as soon as I could
who escaped from the circle of fire
which was engulfing my head—
now all I can feel is a lingering dread.

Mavis's Daughter

Her pasty made-up face
with the smeared rouge
and painted lips
looked even uglier when she
smugly announced to her friend:
and this is Mavis's daughter.
A faint sneer was visible
and I knew what she meant:
daughter of that drunken woman
who sleeps around.
I felt the ignominy of all outcasts.
I felt crippled with shame.
I longed to be someone else's daughter.

And this is Mavis's daughter.
I detested my Mother.
I detested myself.
I detested the judgemental world
that left me wondering: *why me?*
That left me driven by an
unyielding self-destructive urge.
That left me a casualty
of the unkind thoughts of strangers.
That left me being Mavis's daughter forever.

Mavis's Song

In dingy rooms
of old pubs and houses
where smoke hung
like suspended clouds
and the sounds of merriment
echoed through the night
tongues loosed by alcohol
slurred incautious words
and sang salacious songs.

Into these she would come
burdened by a sadness
only she knew.
She was good at hiding her pain.
There was always
something tragic about her.
Her laughter never quite rang true.
Her songs burst forth as though
her life depended upon them.
Her voice, soaring above the others
would break into a drunken lament:
hating him.
hating herself more
because she could not leave him
and love again.

Immaculate Deception

Helen, a friend of my big sister,
often said Mavis was all class.
Mavis always dressed to the nines.
Mavis was elegant and smart.
Mavis would never be seen
in a shabby dress
or worn out shoes.
Mavis was immaculate.

Mavis's house was immaculate too.
On hands and knees
she scrubbed the kitchen floor
every week without fail
waxing and shining its fading lino
with the *Hoover* polisher
which had a mind of its own.
No crumbs or splashes of milk
no vegemite jars or jam tins
no sticky remnants of honey
spoiled her immaculate benches.

Mavis was proud of her house.
It wasn't like Mrs A's
whose table and benches were not immaculate.
They were awash with weeks of debris.
Her floor was lost under rubble
while the clothes basket was
overflowing on the bench.
But she had six kids
and different priorities.

Had a social worker called at our house
they would have had no case to report—
we were clean
our hair didn't have lice
we weren't covered in bruises
our house glowed like a sunbeam.
Our house was so immaculate
the Queen could have called anytime
and eaten her lunch off the floor.

But beneath our spick and span
the dirt was so thick
the mess so profound
we were rank with
the odour of our family
drowning in its own shit.

What Happened to *Madam J?*

How can one reconcile the Queen
who used to hold court in the lounge room
for my brother's student friends
with this ragbag of skin and bone?
How they flocked to your palace
with their enthusiasm for fun.
You were their Queen of Good Times
and what times they were!
The all-night card parties, the grog
the haze of cigarette smoke
wafting through the ambience of the room.
We laughed and drank
we gambled our moneyboxes
we forgot the pain of every day.
You acted the part beautifully, *Madam J.*
Yet all the while you were edging
towards your Armageddon
the alcohol acidifying your moods
bitter words exploding from your lips
showering us with vitriol.
We watched you fall on your own sword.

What happened to *Madam J?*
Your once regal commands
fill a room now empty and silent.

O My Poor Mother

I cannot bear the thought
of you being so feeble
to see you in *that* chair,
that stinking room, by yourself
in the alcohol-induced stupor
with only the TV.

I have had to shut my door
lock my windows
sheathe my heart
to keep you out.
But I always await
the news of your death
hoping you are in a paradise
far away where you rest
in the eye of the storm
and all your drunken yesterdays
are replaced with days of hope and good cheer.

Always there were his phone calls
telling of your falls—
the broken hips
the crushed vertebra
the bruised ribs.
How he delights in your pain.
His smug voice makes me squirm.
I always wonder with a kind of knowing:

did he throw you down the passage
like the last time?

A wave of horror always pricks.
The galling things you suffered before us defy words.
But what terror did he perform in that hovel-house
away from our tear-filled eyes?

The tragedy escalates.
Your family have deserted you
drifting into our own broken lives
and you, alone with him, unprotected
drink to forget.
All we see is the pathetic shell.

I have such dreadful thoughts
that a bullet though your head
would be the kindest thing
I could do for you.
O my poor Mother.

The Day We Found Her

It lingers in me like some strange happening—

When I arrived on an ordinary Sunday
she seemed to be in pain and discomfort

and slumped to ease herself in her chair.
My disdain gave way to concern:

We'll take you to a doctor tomorrow.
Worried, I notified my sister, *Tomorrow then.*

Monday, midday, and the noon swooned
as we arrived on our mission.

Letting ourselves in, a darkness pervaded
the house ghostly in stale stench.

There, in foetal position, whispering into the phone,
she lay like a dying child in the dark, deathly room.

Her nightdress, wrinkled and covered in shit,
clung to her wasted body.

O God, quick, help her! help her!
We grabbed the phone, it was an old friend.

Kath! we have to go, there's something wrong!
She's dying, we're ringing an ambulance!

Pulling her soiled nightdress off, I dressed
her in clean clothes and moved her to another room.

She barely made it, her legs giving way several times,
consciousness ebbing from her quietly.

We gave her all the dignity we could muster
as she lay lapsing away.

I remember that dreadful noon and the panic,
the flurrying around amidst an unfolding tragedy.

Ours was a pathetic attempt to redress the past—
her drink, her men, her stormy world

our obsessive, sad, vitriolic mutterings.
It was a strange happening indeed.

Neglect and self-abuse had taken its toll—
the empty fridge, save for the beer, told a tale.

Then, in hospital, with nobody to guide her soul,
our Mother died two days after

the day we found her.

Irony

Me Mum always said:
*if ya don't eat
ya don't shit,
if ya don't shit
ya die.*
And she did!

JEFFS, Mavis Dorothy—
Passed away on April 21,
1992. Wife of Max (dec.);
loved mother of Marilyn,
Keith and Sandra; loved
Grandma of Brett, Jason
and Fiona.

Privately cremated at
Ballarat on April 23.

Mother I Watched

You lived excessively
I watched
You smoked excessively
I watched
You got drunk excessively
I watched
You became lonely excessively
I watched
You starved yourself excessively
I watched
You became ill excessively
I watched
You died excessively
I watched
and feel my guilt excessively

No Tears

No tears for you, Mother.
No weeping into soggy handkerchiefs
by the gathered few
who view your elevated coffin
festooned with perfunctory flowers.

No tears for you, Mother
who drifted out of our lives years ago
when you abandoned the world
for a ramshackle chair set in the corner of
the stale room you barely shadowed.

No tears for you, Mother.
No great wails of grief.
No weighty outpourings
to mark your passing.
Death snatched you long ago.

But much has changed.
Emotions have swelled enormously.
Thoughts of you filter through my mind
moment after moment.
So deep and compelling that
the tears have more than been shed
they have flowed and flowed
the dry eyes have become torrents.

re Estate M.D. Jeffs deceased

This now completes...
>The words catch in my throat
>my tongue is tethered.

the administration of...
>She has gone and is now a mere
>source of leftover assets.

your late...
>I am thankful for small mercies
>but feel the finality is unbearable.

mother's...
>I choke on the realities of death
>as this moment presses the air from my lungs.

estate.
>She is parcelled up
>signed, sealed and delivered
>disposed of legally
>carved up in a document
>the woman who birthed me
>the woman whose motherless mothering
>left me pregnantly empty
>except to say:

>Rest peacefully in arms that caress you
>Mavis Dorothy Jeffs (nee Bryant)
>18/9/1923—21/4/1992

I Mourn You Dead, Mother

Once upon a time I willed you dead.
Now I mourn you dead.
I thought you were indestructible
surviving it all—
the abuse of your body
the torment of your soul
you even saw him into his inferno.

I mourn your last years and months.
I mourn your last days and hours.
I mourn your last breath.

I mourn you more than I expected
the grief is belated
the cup overflows.

I shall keep a quiet vigil
over your faint light in my heart
while I mourn you dead.

Anniversary

They tell me how
beautiful you were
but I could not
believe their stories
when I saw how your
body had wasted away
when I saw how your
breasts were no more.

I remember your sunken face
and gnarled bones.
I remember your withered skin.
I remember you dancing on the edge
of your alcoholic razor blade every day
your wounds never healing.
I remember you being
an alien I did not know.

It is two years since I
delivered you to the flames
and still you hover
the haggard bleeding phantom
who haunts my mind.

Guilt

Re-reading my words
which will haunt me
written in times of a bitterness
that consumed my soul
I see a rage had smouldered.

A rage as powerful as
his tirades and beatings of you
that saw his face flame scarlet
with the blood vessels
distended on his neck.

My rage was muted
                inward
                    twisted.

There was a time when I went blind.

I saw too late
                after death
                    after the fact
            after I had assessed history
and found myself guilty of
                    Mother-hatred.

It makes me qualmish
to the guts.

Mother, I wish I could see you again
        to let you judge me
                for the neglect.

Feline Love

For Patricia Sykes

When a feline beauty
curls its furred body
upon my lap
smooching its elegance
lounging languidly in the midst
of my curious enduring love
I think of you, Mum.
In every fickle feline sovereign
that has graced my home
there has been a piece of you
an undying reservoir of love
that has overflowed with a raucous joy.

I have devoured your joy of cats.
This tiny morsel of you
affords a deep connection
to your lost soul.
I sit in the calm and stroke
the smooth fur of a purring majesty.
I draw your beckoning soul's
outstretched hand to mine.
I grasp this transcendence;
it is all I have left of
the wasteland that was you.

Crazy Woman Survivor

Sorrow will slide
down gutters of fine print.
At dusk, a rushing whiteness
will seize and hold you safe.

Gwen Harwood

Crazy Woman

Crazy woman looks back
on her crazy life
in that crazy home
with her crazy parents
doing crazy things
yet no one thought them crazy.

Crazy woman sits huddled
with her crazy thoughts
and crazy voices
talks crazy words
to the crazy people
and everyone knows she's crazy.

Crazy woman wasn't always crazy
and wonders in her crazy mind
why she went crazy
and sees crazy shrinks
while her crazy family
drove everyone crazy.

The Quest

For Virginia

All my lingering years
I have lived in the wake
of your putrefying lives,
washing myself over and over obsessively
to remove the stench of your barbarism;
scrubbing vigorously my crawling skin
until its rawness craved a soothing balm.
Bearing witness was unbearable.
Even when I averted my eyes
I still saw, more clearly than before,
the hell you dragged from
the nether regions into our home
that made us quake in our beds,
its fires charring our dreams
into blackened nightmares.
My imagination could not
invent a scene more gruelling
than the play you acted before us.
And what do I say or do
with all this inside me
even with the satisfaction
of knowing you are no longer?
All my lingering years
years of fire, years of tempests and madness,
I have quested to find my humanity—
a deep sustaining humanity,
the only balm to soothe my soul's craving
for a life unburdened, untroubled and free.

Baggage

The house of cards in which
we lived our awful lives
fell away in bits—
the Ace of Love here
the Queen of Peace there
all the cards, one by one,
folding and crumbling.

Even when the days
were full of child's play
I was milked of the thing
that connects me to the world
and I became entangled
in your cobweb of dysphoria,
its spiders sucking me dry.

I am fearful of your ghosts
lurking in the dark wood
through which I stumble
on a road to somewhere
hauling enough baggage
for a trip to infinity.

Favourite Aunt

For Auntie June

You looked on silently
as I hauled the load.

You looked on silently
while I lied impassively
in front of your comforting fire.

You looked on silently
as I cowered inside.

You looked on silently
wanting to take me away
from their putrid cage.

You looked on silently
unable to penetrate my darkness.

You looked on silently
your wordless love touching me
as I struggled.

with a loneliness that did not die
while you looked on silently.

Strange Homecoming

For Marilyn

For a faint smudge of make-up
on the dirty face washer
he yelled at you: *filthy bitch!*
tossing it in your face
like you were a piece of dirt.
He was always cursing you,
hurling you down the front steps
like a rag doll.
And you, in like manner,
vowing never to return,
your anger as powerful as his.
Those days, long gone,
remain as clear as yesterday.
I could never have stood up to him like you.
It was a clash of titans
when you crossed swords;
you were as willful as he
just as quick to anger.

Yet, at the end,
it was you who saw him to his slumber,
sharing his final moments
while the rest of us fled:
*you old bastard, you've gone and done
what you promised you'd never do to me!*
He had left you with her.

Strange things families
full of inscrutable alliances.
You were forgiving of his maniacal evil.
I was less generous.
You mellowed your hatred.
I was unforgiving in my distance.
You found love
while I seethed
like a cauldron of caustic chemicals
pondering your strange homecoming
to his deathbed.

Little Boy/Troubled Man

For Keith

Little boy shedding tears
hiding under his bed.

Little boy standing tall
protecting her from him.

Little boy who saw her
in the arms of other men.

Little boy craving the watchful eye
of the father who neglected you.

Little boy forced to grow
into a man too soon.

Little boy whose wings were clipped
on the threshold of selfhood.

Troubled man fearful of having
a temper like his.

Troubled man too afraid
to have children of his own.

Troubled man lost for words
unable to talk of his emotions.

Troubled man who seeks respite
from the memories of his childhood.

Troubled man
peace be with you.

Mother A

For Coralie

You were the tower
with six children
and a husband who sat by the heater
in his underpants in the kitchen
who didn't care who was there
how he looked
what he did
drank himself into a stupor
went out all night
spewed his guts out in the morning.
We all thought he was crazy.
It was the war that did him in.

You were the tower
the one who held it all together
surviving his violence and craziness
his head jammed in the gas oven
the police carting him off to the loony bin.

You stood tall amidst all this
making cakes, drop scones
marshmallows, toffees and coconut ice
for charity stalls and clubs.
Playing piano for the callisthenics girls
the marching girls, the senior cits
and our sing-a-longs.

Your children scattered
to the baying wolves
building new lives
in the reach of your anchor.
I too was of the Diaspora
finding a home in the hills
we call Christmas
where birds offer treasures
and flowers carpet my floor.
When you arrive
a card greeting the season
a breath of old air
blows in from another time.
You stand luminous again
a faint shaft of light
to calm the heaving seas
where my nightmares wrestle
with my dreams.

Letting Go

So much to do today:
kill memory, kill pain,
turn heart into stone,
and yet prepare to live again.

Anna Akhmatova

Sometimes I look back in anger
unable to *kill memory, kill pain.*
It was more difficult
when you were always on my breath.
My tongue got tired from lashing you.
Time has done its thing.
Death has done its thing.
I feel a distance
almost a numbness.
You rest silently in
the cold of death's shadow
and I cherish the moments
when I can say: *that was then.*

Damage Control

My siblings and I
were given into the world
unprotected and damaged.
I always wanted
to warn those around me
to beware of damaged people;
to beware of me.
Hard as I try to plough the torrid waters
and steer a safe course
often my boat crashes upon rocks,
the wreckage floating onto
someone else's once uncluttered shore.
I wonder if anyone is able to live
doing as little damage as possible.
Yet in spite of my tremulous misgivings
and fears of harmfulness to others
my instincts have driven me
to seek the company of strangers;
to reach out further
than I ever wanted,
to cling tightly to the friends
I desperately need.
If nothing else, I am a survivor.
After all these years
I cannot deny this truth.
I am a survivor!

What Have I Done?

I have told the world about you
a dark and brooding story
convulsing with aftershock fall-out.
Love and hate enlace and
truth lies buried.

I should like to have told a grand tale
of jaunty family strolls down everglades
delighting in unceasing requited love
or of serene, lazy days unburdened
by aftermaths of turbulent nights before.

O I should like my story to have
been many things it is not!
Instead, dirty linen hangs limp
on a corroding line soon to collapse.
Instead, a tangled tapestry
of unravelling thread
strangles my needle
and the cloth has no definition.
Odds and ends hang defiantly.

Mum and Dad, you are elusive
to my questing mind's eye.
My imagination has wrought a tale
dramatic and grotesque.
Was it really as I have said?
Surely these are the ravings of a madwoman!
I cannot believe my words
which scour the pages
like Frankenstein's raging monster.
What have I done?

In Memoriam

JEFFS—Max and Mavis.
  Time passes, lives
  change, but memories
  will always remain.—
  Sandra, Marilyn and
  Keith.

OTHER BOOKS FROM SPINIFEX PRESS

Sandy Jeffs
Poems from the Madhouse

This is disturbing but quite wonderful poetry, because of its clarity, its humour, its imagery, and the insights it gives us into being human, being made, being sane. I read and read—and was profoundly moved. I delighted in it as poetry; I was touched by its honesty, courage and vulnerability.

Anne Deveson

The language challenges her with fifty names for madness, writing of a life of vigilance and struggle, she enlarges our understanding of human capacity.   Judith Rodriguez

Certificate of Commendation, Human Rights Award for Poetry, 1994
Second Prize, Anne Elder FAW Award, 1994

Deborah Staines
Now Millennium

Deborah Staines' respect for and awareness of language's dynamic possibilities bring inner and outer worlds attentively alive.   Fay Zwicky

This book is really wild ... There's so much passion and commitment there and she's drunk with words.

Dorothy Hewett

Winner, Mary Gilmore Award, 1994
ISBN 1 875559 20 5

Nina Mariette
Painting Myself In

An account of recovery from sexual abuse through creativity:

*When I paint I can move myself to a space of freedom that I've
never felt before.*   Nina Mariette

ISBN 1 875559 73 6

Susan Hawthorne
Bird

*Many-eyed and many-lived is this poet, as seismologist or
lover, bird or newborn child. To the classic figures of Sappho
or Eurydice she brings all the Now! Here! sense of discovery
that fires her modern girl taking lessons in flight.*

Judith Rodriguez

ISBN 1 875559 88 4

Patricia Sykes
Wire Dancing

In poems that are at once allusive and elusive, Sykes leaps like an
acrobat between past and present, mythology and history, the
everyday and the exotic, from Bosnia to the circus. And, dancing
nimbly along the high wires of emotion and intellect, she is
passionate, witty, erudite and ironic.

ISBN 1 875559 90 5

Suniti Namjoshi
Feminist Fables

An ingenious reworking of fairytales. Mythology mixed with the author's original material and vivid imagination. An indispensable feminist classic.

Her imagination soars to breathtaking heights.
                                        Kerry Lyon, *Australian Book Review*
ISBN 1 875559 19 1

Suniti Namjoshi
St Suniti and the Dragon

Ironic, fantastic, elegant and elegaic, fearful and funny. A thoroughly modern fable.

It's hilarious, witty, elegantly written, hugely inventive, fantastic, energetic.   U.A. Fanthorpe
ISBN 1 875559 18 3

Diane Fahey
The Body in Time

Diane Fahey pieces together a world—with integrity and incomparable delicacy—much as the fragile light of a star defines a universe.   Annie Greet
ISBN 1 875559 37 X

Jordie Albiston
Nervous Arcs

Jordie Albiston writes with sharp intelligence, lyrical grace, and moral passion. A name to watch for.

Janette Turner Hospital

Winner, Mary Gilmore Award, 1996
Second Prize, Anne Alder FAW Award, 1996
ISBN 1 875559 37 X

Louise Crisp
Ruby Camp

Crisp's insights and perceptions are so original and intense that she has needed to find a new language, precise and sensuous, mysterious and revealing, held in a fine balance of rhythm and phrasing. She creates a radically new way of 'knowing' the East Gippsland bush: 'strong as illusion the dream works/ its way into landscape'. It is finally a book about joy. Marie Tulip

Miriel Lenore
Travelling Alone Together

Three journeys across the Nullarbor and time are interwoven as Lenore explores our myths.

This poet/traveller is incredibly modest and respectful of what is given her to experience. She travels across her many landscapes naming without appropriating. Alison Clark
ISBN 1 875559 83 3